MODERN
ARCHERY

*A Complete Handbook to the Sport and
Guide to the Making and Care of Equipment*

by

FRANK L. BILSON

*British Champion, 1948/9
Captain of Targets, Royal Toxophilite Society,
Master Bowman and Vice-President,
Grand National Archery
Society*

*With fifteen illustrations and numerous
working diagrams*

THE 91st GRAND NATIONAL ARCHERY MEETING IN THE GROUNDS OF WORCESTER COLLEGE, OXFORD, 1938.

Preface

THE brief handbook entitled ENGLISH ARCHERY published by the present writer some two years ago met with so wide a welcome that it became evident that it was fulfilling the purpose that prompted its issue. The opportunity has therefore been taken to rewrite and revise that booklet and to add considerably more matter based on increased experience of his own needs, as well as of the needs of others possibly more recently introduced to the fascinating sport of Archery.

No attempt is made to deal exhaustively with the many interesting problems and side-issues connected with the sport; the writer has merely sought to put down as briefly and conveniently as possible the information he himself has culled from many and varied sources, the chief of which is, naturally enough, his own experience. His hope is that others may become interested in this fascinating sport, and even that those who are already Archers may not find this little book unworthy of their notice, but that they may be helped to more successful enjoyment of their shooting.

The comradeship and willing help of fellow-archers is one of the great joys of the sport which the writer wishes gratefully to acknowledge. Among the many who have helped him with advice and experience, he wishes to mention particularly the following: E. H. Nelson, Weston Martyr, Col. Temperley and H. A. Titcomb of the Royal Toxophilite Society; Dr. Elmer and Prof. Klopsteg of the U.S.A.; also Mr. and Mrs. Nettleton and Capt. R. W. Pinchback. He is also grateful to the Editor of *Sport and Country* for his permission to make use of the copyright photographs of the writer illustrating shooting technique.

F.L.B.

Contents

The Story of the Bow

THE bow must have been one of the very earliest inventions of man, for great numbers of flint arrowheads have been found in several parts of the world. Many of these are undoubtedly connected with remains of the Early Stone Age. The bows and arrows themselves being of wood have rarely survived, but two examples were found in Switzerland which experts claim to date from the Later Stone Age.

The first authentic mention of archery in historic times is found in Gen. 21: 20, where we are told that Ishmael became an archer. Esau, too, was evidently an accomplished archer, as he was in the habit of shooting deer with his bow to replenish the family larder.

When we come to the time of King Saul we find that not only do archers form an effective part of the Philistine army, but there were no doubt many who enjoyed the sport for the healthy outdoor exercise it afforded. We see from I Sam 20: 18-22, that it was quite a usual thing for Jonathan to shoot at a " mark " or target, probably at a considerable range, as he needed a boy to fetch his arrows.

King David was quick to see the advantage of archery in peace and war, for " he bade them teach the children of Judah the use of the bow " (II Sam. 1: 18).

In addition to a number of other references in Scripture to the widespread use and love of the bow, there are very many records in writing and in sculpture telling of the prowess of great men of old with this weapon. One of the royal sports of Assyria was lion-shooting from a chariot. This is very clearly depicted in a bas-relief of Asshur-na-zirpal who is seen to have already shot one lion and with his arrow drawn to the point aimed at another about to leap at him in the chariot. Big game hunting of this type obviously needs a strong and efficient bow and accurate shooting, although it is by no means beyond the power of modern archers and equipment. Only a few years back an American, Arthur Young, made a trip to Africa, and on foot shot full-grown lions with his bow, using a sharp broadhead arrow similar to the old English war arrow.

While the Africans and Western Europeans used bows of wood, the Greeks and more Eastern nations developed a very efficient composite bow of horn, wood, and sinew.

It is thought that the Scandinavians first introduced the long bow into Britain, and although there is no doubt that archers were used on both sides at the Battle of Hastings, yet it is certain that in that battle and after it the Normans demonstrated the great advantage of the long bow in war.

Following the Conquest, the peasants and yeomen of these islands quickly became proficient in handling the long bow, and for many centuries they formed the backbone of every English army. Those interested in history will know that the battles of Falkirk in 1298, Crecy in 1346, Poitiers in 1356, and Agincourt in 1415 were all won chiefly through the superiority of the English long bow.

Because of this many of our kings promoted laws to encourage the practice of archery as a sport, particularly the shooting at long ranges, over 200 yards, and at " Rovers " or a series of marks of unknown distances apart where the range must be carefully judged. For centuries archery was the one outdoor sport loved and practiced by the vast majority of Englishmen, and some became great experts in the distance and accuracy of their shooting. Among these the most famous of course are Robin Hood and his Merry Men, although a few of the feats ascribed to him by tradition are, to say the least, exaggerations.

Some of our kings became expert archers themselves, and Henry VIII on the " Field of the Cloth of Gold " gave a demonstration of his skill which we are told astonished the French nobility present. About this time Roger Ascham wrote his famous book on archery, *Toxophilus,* and described his " five points " for " goode shutynge " which we will discuss later.

As time went on special fields were set apart for the practice of archery with marks at varying but known distances, very much after the pattern of a modern golf course. Such a course were the " Finsbury Fields " outside the City of London, which stretched from the city wall to as far as the Angel, Islington. One body of archers shooting on these Fields were officially formed into the Honorable Artillery Company, " artillery " being the old name for bows and arrows. This famous British Regiment still have their headquarters near Moorgate, and the International Archery Tournament was shot in the " fields " adjoining their headquarters in 1938, the long distance championship being won on that occasion by an Englishman, C. J. Smith, of Chelmsford.

Back in 1780 the remaining members of the Archery Section of the H.A.C. helped to form a club known as the Toxophilite Society. From this time and for a hundred years archery as a sport grew in popularity, due no doubt partly to the fact that it is one of the finest exercises for developing the chest and lungs in the open air.

King George IV took an interest in the sport and honoured the leading London Society with his patronage, thus making it the Royal Toxophilite Society, which still has the honour of the present King as patron. This Club, with the Woodmen of Arden, who shoot at Meriden near Coventry, and the Royal Company of Archers, who still form the official King's bodyguard in Edinburgh, are recognised as the three leading clubs among the hundred or more archery clubs in this country. In America this fascinating sport and hobby is far more popular and is fast becoming one of the recognised national sports.

Beside the instructive hobby of making one's own bow and arrows, etc., there are so many different kinds of shooting which give the sport its appeal to every sort of temperament. There is Flight Shooting which strives solely for the longest possible distance; an arrow has been shot over 900 yards! There is roving — shooting at a series of odd marks whilst walking through the fields. There is modern archery golf ; and a match between an archer and a golfer makes a very close game. There is hunting for game big and small, from lions in Africa to rabbits in England. And there is the competitive target shooting at short and long ranges which require all the strength, nerve and skill a man possesses.

THE ADVANTAGES OF ARCHERY AS A SPORT

Archery has several advantages over many other sports. First of all, large or small numbers can take part, with equal enjoyment. Also in target shooting archers always record their scores so that even an individual archer shoots not only against his own best score but also against the known score of others. This naturally leads to keen competition and a continual effort to correct faults of technique.

Another advantage is that special clothing is not needed so long as sleeves are kept out of the way of bowstrings. This is usually done by wearing a leather guard known as a " bracer," which also protects the arm from the recoil of the string.

With a hall or passage allowing 20 yards or more it is also possible to arrange archery indoors during the winter months, and the 24in. target is ideal for this type of shooting.

Even those physically unfit for any other sport can find enjoyment in archery. One young fellow with his left arm off at the elbow had a special attachment fitted to his bow and shot quite well in that way.

One of the best British archers, with whom the writer has often had the pleasure of shooting, lost a leg a few years ago when his fighter plane crashed. The writer also knows of one man, crippled in both legs, who shoots while sitting on a stool. His friends are very happy to retrieve his arrows for him. Archery has also been found helpful in at least four hospitals in Britain for paraplegics, who are quite able to shoot while sitting in their wheeled chairs.

At the shorter ranges, up to 60 yards, age makes very little difference to success. The important thing is to use a bow well within one's control, so that it can be held perfectly steady at full draw after many repeated shots.

As in all sports, perseverance and practice are needed to develop the muscles and master the correct technique. When that is achieved no sport is more healthy and enjoyable.

Competition Rounds

M ODERN archery in Britain chiefly takes the form of competitive target shooting, and is based on given numbers of arrows known as "rounds." In Britain and America the National Tournaments are decided upon the York Round for men and the Hereford or National Rounds for women.

The York Round was instituted in 1844 when the Grand National was first shot at York. It consists of 72 arrows at 100 yards range, 48 arrows at 80 yards, and 24 arrows at 60 yards, on the 4ft. target designed in 1792 for H.R.H. Prince George, then Prince of Wales. Actually only six arrows are used and are shot over and over again. The archer first shoots three arrows from the shooting line, then steps back to let his target mates shoot their first three. After which they shoot in turn their second three before walking to the target to record the score and retrieve their arrows. Having shot six dozen arrows in this way he takes his stand at 80 yards and then at 60 yards until the whole 144 arrows have been shot. For this round it is customary to use a bow with a 45-50 lbs. pull, so that one can easily understand the need for physical fitness to shoot through a York Round.

Some British clubs also shoot the American round consisting of 30 arrows each at 60 yards, 50 yards and 40 yards. This round, of course, takes less time than the York and can conveniently be shot by men and women together.

A trophy presented by Col. Clive Temperley — known as the "Ascham Mazer" — goes to the archer who makes the highest American round score shot under American rules (6 arrows to an end, shot one way) in club tournaments. This "Ascham Mazer" is the counterpart of a similar trophy for the York round shot under the old English rules (3 arrows each way) in America. The old English methods are considered to be about 100 points harder than the American methods in a York round.

The most popular competition for ladies is the Western

round: four dozen arrows at 60 yards and four dozen at 50 yards. A more strenuous competition for ladies is the Hereford round: six dozen arrows at 80 yards, four dozen at 60 yards and two dozen at 50 yards. They also shoot the National Round, four dozen at 60 yards and two dozen at 50 yards.

A COMPETITION SCORE

Score sheet of the British Record York Round, shot by F. L. Bilson on August 18th, 1948, in competition at the Royal Toxophilite Society's Ground.

6 dozen at 100 yards —

				Hits	Score	Golds
3	955	975	775	10	62	2
755	9	555	53	9	49	1
333	71	975	771	11	53	1
995	973	71	753	11	65	3
771	51	777	55	10	52	
773	31	551	751	11	45	
		Total at 100 yards		62	326	7

4 dozen at 80 yards —

775	733	977	933	12	70	2
995	973	977	753	12	80	4
775	953	995	955	12	78	4
755	995	975	773	12	78	3
		Total at 80 yards		48	306	13

2 dozen at 60 yards —

755	771	975	755	12	70	1
755	777	75	753	11	65	
		Total at 60 yards		23	135	1
	Grand Total, Single York Round			133	767	21

The above was shot under the old rules (3 arrows, two ways). The new six arrows one way shooting was adopted by the Grand National Archery Society in March, 1949.

Bow-Making

THE secrets of bow and arrow making have been closely guarded for centuries by the professional bowyers and fletchers. As far as the writer knows, this is the first time detailed instructions for these interesting crafts have been published in this country.

Anyone moderately good at carpentry should not find great difficulty in making his own tackle provided the following principles and directions are followed closely.

Good bow-woods are at present scarce in Britain. Spanish or Italian yew is best but almost unobtainable. English yew is not nearly so good. In either case the yew staves must be seasoned for three or four years. Also as the grain must be carefully followed so that the light sapwood is not cut into, yew is really the wood for the professional bowyer rather than the amateur.

The best wood for the amateur bowyer to use is degame, otherwise known as lemonwood. Well seasoned staves of this can be obtained from certain timber importers. The grain is so fine that it can be ignored. Hickory will make a bow but as it is rather slow in recoil it does not give very good cast. Seasoned ash is rather similar but is more liable to break unless the bow is very long for the length of draw. While all bow-woods must be well seasoned they should not be allowed to get bone dry and so become too brittle.

The general principles always to be borne in mind when making a bow are these:

1. There should be no bend in the region of the handle. This must therefore be thick enough to be rigid.

2. Each limb should bend in an even, smooth curve throughout its length (see Fig. 7). To secure this a sharp plane should be used as much as possible, when making a lemonwood bow, rather than a spokeshave which may tend to make thin, weak spots leading to breakage. Work with the grain as far as possible.

3.   The upper limb should be 2in. longer than the lower limb in the traditional bow.   This will allow the arrow to be shot from nearer the centre of the bow and makes the lower limb stiffer which is desirable in the traditional type of bow.

4.   It is a fact that the shorter the bow the greater the pull needed to draw it ; the thickness being equal. ᴖ It is therefore suggested that those beginning archery should make bows longer than necessary.   These should be well within their powers to draw continually to the full length of an arrow (26in. or 28in. according to height).   When their muscles are more developed and accustomed to the bow and they feel they can manage a stronger weapon, it will be a simple matter to cut an inch or so off each end.   This will also increase the " cast " or shooting power.

5.   If the stave to be used has a decided and even bend it is an advantage to use the concave surface as the " back " (surface held away from archer).   This will mean that all the wood will be cut from the convex side.   The bow will thus remain straighter after it has been used a little, as lemonwood tends to " follow the string."

MAKING THE TRADITIONAL BOW

A stave 6ft. long and 1in. by 1in. is required.   First find the centre of the stave (C in Fig. 1) by measurement, then 1in. above this and 3in. below draw lines round the four sides of the stave as at A and B, Fig. 1.   This gives 4in. for the handle.   After determining which is the side most free from flaws, etc., or the concave side in the case of a bent stave, mark this side " back." No wood will be cut away from the back.   On either side adjacent to the back, draw straight lines from A to E and B to F (Fig. 2), allowing for a thickness of 3/8in. at E and F.   Then, with a sharp plane, take off the surplus wood above these lines.

Now turn the stave completely over so that the back is uppermost.   Draw two diagonal lines from corner to corner of the handle.   Where these intersect will be the exact centre of the handle.   Using thin string drawn taut or the edge of a long straight board, a straight line must now be drawn from end to end of the stave passing through the exact centre of the handle. It will not matter if the stave is slightly warped so long as 3/16in. of wood can be allowed on each side of this centre line at E and F. This centre line will help you to ensure that the bow is true when

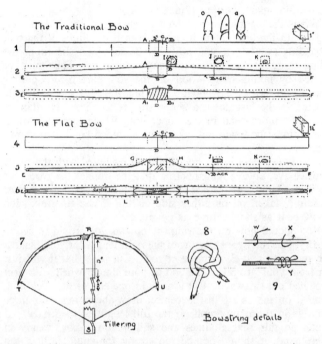

The Traditional Bow

The Flat Bow

Tillering

Bowstring details

finished, which is very important.

Having made marks at E and F 3/16in. on either side of the centre line, draw straight lines from A and A1 to these marks at E, and from B and B1 to these marks at F (as in Fig. 3). Now turn the stave on its side and plane away surplus wood.

The bow will now be roughly rectangular in section throughout its length. Still using the plane, take the edges off and gradually round the bow as at sections I, J and K in Fig. 2. The back must be left much flatter than the other three sides. A small piece of wood should be glued on the handle at D and then can be rounded with a file. Before finishing and fitting the handle covering, temporary nocks should be cut at E and F with a small rat-tail file or a penknife. A string should then be fitted (see "Bow Strings") and the bow "tillered" as in Fig. 7. The tillering board R—S consists of a stout piece of wood about 30in. long. It has a large V cut at the top and small notches cut down one side, 3in. apart, starting 13in. from R.

When the handle of the bow is placed in the V, and the string put in the first notch, it can be seen if the limbs of the bow are bending evenly. It will probably be seen that the limbs are bending more at the ends than anywhere else. This must be corrected by taking more wood off the stiff part before putting the string on the second notch. Continue this process until with the string in the last notch a shape similar to Fig. 7 is attained, with a little more bend in the upper limb R—U than the lower. The traditional bow will not take quite so much bend as is shown in figure 7.

Any unevenness in the bend must be regulated with the plane or spokeshave, always remembering that the thinner the wood the more it will bend. If there is a weakness at one spot, wood must be carefully taken off on either side of it. When tillering, keep the bow bent as short a time as possible.

You should now try drawing the bow as you would in shooting. If you haven't yet an arrow of the right length for you, make a rough one with a stick or piece of rod. Cut it so that it will just reach from your armpit to the end of your thumb when your arm is stretched out sideways. Cut a nock in one end of the stick and, placing it on the string in the centre, draw the string with three fingers (as in the photograph) to the full length of the arrow. If you can do this several times and still hold the bow steady in the left hand, it should not be too strong for you. If it is too strong, plane more wood off until the shape and pull or " weight " of the bow suits you. Now, if you have a scraper (Rawlplug or plain steel type) use this to remove tool marks, getting down to a nice finish with first coarse, and then fine, glass-paper or steel wool. Finally, cut permanent nocks as at O, P and Q. " O " is the back held away from the archer when shooting and " Q " towards the archer. " P " is side view with a small hole in the upper limb for the " string-keeper." When the nocks are free from rough edges likely to cut or wear the string, the final finish can be put on. French polish is best, two or three coats can be rubbed on with a rag as it dries quickly. Rub down with fine glass paper after the first coat. Polish with a soft rag. The handle may be covered with a leather thong glued and bound round with the ends tapered and tucked in. Some prefer a cord binding set in glue.

MAKING THE FLAT BOW

A stave of lemonwood 6ft. 9in. or 10in. is best so that 12in. can be cut off one end and become the handle riser (see G—H, Fig. 5).

One of the wide surfaces must be chosen as the back. The concave side of the stave is best. Then find the centre by measurement and mark off the handle 1in. above and 3in. below (Fig. 4), also draw centre line as for the traditional bow. In this case, however, the nocks will be ½in. wide, so ¼in. must be allowed on each side of the centre line at E and F (see Fig. 6). Now 7in. from centre of handle draw lines across back at L and M (Fig. 6), and from the ends of these lines draw straight lines to the marks ¼in. on either side of centre line at E and F.

The stave can now be turned on its side and the wood outside these lines planed away.

The handle-riser should now be fitted. It saves time to cut the corners off with a saw as indicated by dotted lines at G and H (Fig. 5). The riser can then be carefully glued on with 6in. on either side of the centre of the handle D. Casein glue can be used provided the makers' directions are carefully followed.

Otherwise, warm the surfaces to be glued and use "Seccotine" or hot glue, and leave in a vice or clamps for 24 hours. Or bind tightly with cord if you haven't a vice, etc. As an added precaution it is wise to drill a hole and fit a stout screw in the centre when glue is dry, as this joint must take a great strain.

The next job is to bring the stave down to the required thickness. Some may prefer to do this before glueing on the handleriser. Two inches on either side of the centre of the handle is the full 1½in. thick, then a steep slope down to ¾in. at 6in. from centre and tapering off to 5/8in. at 8in., ½in. half way along the limb and 3/8in. at the ends (see Fig. 5). These are rough thicknesses which can be varied according to the required weight (*i.e.*, pull) of the bow. Mark out each side before cutting away spare wood.

The curve near the handle will need to be formed with a spokeshave. Use a plane, however, as soon as it is possible.

The narrow portion of the handle should now be marked out on the back in pencil, allowing a thickness of ¾in. for two inches on either side of the handle centre D, then gradually widen out to the full 1¼in. at L and M (see Fig. 6). The edges of the

bow should now be rounded to a shape similar to the sections at
J and K in Fig. 5.   Finally tiller, cut the nocks, and finish your
bow as instructions given for the traditional type.   The handle
can be covered with a piece of leather 3in. or 4in. wide glued on
with the join at the front.

DIMENSIONS FOR SYMMETRICALLY BALANCED FLAT BOWS, WITH LIMBS OF RECTANGULAR SECTION

This table of figures was worked out by Forest Nagler of the
U.S.A. and can be used for any weight (pull) of bows from 25 lbs.
to 78 lbs. in yew, or proportionately heavier if degame or osage-
orange is used.

A straight centre line should be drawn along a 5ft. 8in. stave
and half the width given marked on either side of that line.   When
these marks are joined they form the outline of the bow.   The bow
should then be worked down to the thickness given in tables and
tillered and finished as directed on Pages 15 and 16.

Distances from Ends in inches	Width of Limb			Thickness of Limb			
	A	B	C	1	2	3	4
0	.47	.37	.30	.41	.37	.35	.33
4	.94	.75	.56	.50	.44	.40	.36
8	1.33	1.06	.78	.57	.51	.46	.41
12	1.43	1.13	.84	.65	.57	.52	.47
16	1.50	1.19	.88	.71	.63	.57	.52
20	1.58	1.25	.93	.76	.68	.61	.55
24	1.63	1.30	.96	.80	.71	.64	.58
28	1.70	1.35	1.00	.83	.73	.66	.60
29	1.62	1.30	.97	.87	.78	.71	.65
30	1.40	1.05	.90	.95	.90	.85	.80
31	.95	.87	.80	1.30	1.20	1.10	1.00
32	.87	.80	.75	1.60	.50	1.40	1.30
34	.87	.80	.75	1.60	1.50	1.40	1.30

(28–34: Handle Dips)

Weights of Bows Based on Widths				
	A	78 lbs.	62 lbs.	50 lbs.	41 lbs.
	B	62 lbs.	49 lbs.	40 lbs.	33 lbs.
	C	46 lbs.	37 lbs.	30 lbs.	25 lbs.

Bowstrings

THE best bowstrings have been made for centuries by a few family craftsmen in Belgium. In spite of many attempts, "stringers" of other countries have not yet been able to equal in quality and finish these Flemish hemp bowstrings.

Satisfactory strings can, however, be made from any good linen thread which does not stretch. Cable-type fishing line is good and it is usually marked with the breaking strain on the spool. Whatever thread or line is used, it is wise to find this out. A sufficient number of threads must be taken to make their combined breaking strain add up to about 200 lbs. (150 lbs. for a 30 lb. bow). For example, if using a line with a 10 lb. breaking strain, 20 lines should be used.

Cut the strands 18ins. longer than the bow for which they are intended. In forming the top loop it is first necessary to taper the ends of the strands with a knife. Having done this, divide the number of strands into two equal groups and wax each group thoroughly with beeswax for about a foot. Now hold the full number of strands between the thumb and first finger of the left hand about 10ins. from the end and with the right hand twist tightly to the right one of the two groups and turn it over the other one to the left (towards you). Now twist the second group to the right and turn this over the first one to the left. Continue twisting to the right and turning over to the left each group in turn until about 3ins. has been twisted for the loop.

The remaining few inches of one group of strands is now placed with half the number of strands in the main string and waxed together. Also the other short group is placed along the remaining long group. Thus the loop is formed and the process of twisting to the right and turning over to the left must now be continued with the new groups made up of the short and long strands.

Gradually the tapered ends will be lost in the main string and if the tapering and twisting has been done properly no ends should show, merely the original group of long strands remains with a neat strong loop at the top. These main strands should now be well waxed and after straightening them out to ensure an even tension they should be twisted to the left (anti-clockwise) for say 30 to 40 turns. Too many turns may weaken the string instead of strengthening it. The wax is then well rubbed in by using a piece of leather folded between the fingers. The friction melts the wax into the string.

To strengthen the lower end of the string a number of strengthening strands should be cut about one foot long and about half the number of the main strands. These must be tapered with a knife at one end and well waxed.

The main strands are then divided into two equal groups at the bottom and half the number of strengthening strands placed with each group so that the ends not tapered come flush with the ends of the main strands. Each group of strands is now twisted to the right and turned over the other to the left as was done to form the top loop, but in this case no loop is formed. If the twisting is commenced high enough up the main string the tapered ends of the strengthening strands will be completely hidden. Continue the twisting to the bottom and then secure the ends with a few turns of thread.

A NEW METHOD

You will need a piece of board (B) just about the same length as your bow. Fix a three inch peg of $\frac{1}{2}$in. dowel rod (P) in one end of the board and over this peg put the top loop of your old string. Stretch the old string along the board and put another 3in. peg (P) through the bottom loop and fix this peg into the board. The pegs will now give you the exact length for your new strings.

On one peg tie loosely one end of the thread, then wind round from peg to peg until you have the required number of threads as above. Now undo the original end and tie it in a reef knot (K) to the end you have left. The knot should be just at the peg.

You now have one continuous circle of threads running loosely round the pegs. With a pencil make a mark on each section of the threads at (M) one inch from each peg. Then slip the threads round until those four marks come opposite each other at the centre of the board. The threads between these marks will become the loops to go over the nocks of the bow, so some whipping or serving

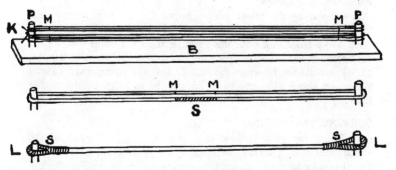

B. BOARD.   M. MARKS ON THREADS.   P. PEGS.
S. SERVING FOR LOOPS.   K. KNOT.   L. LOOPS.

(S) must be put on between the two marks on each section.   It makes a better looking string if this serving is done with thin, coloured string or heavy thread.   Red or green looks quite well.

The served parts are then slid back to the pegs and adjusted evenly round them.   With the same string or thread as used for the serving, bind the two sections together for about two inches, thus forming the loops (L).

The string can now be taken off the pegs and it should be twisted a few times before it is put on the bow.   As this type of string has fixed loops at both ends any adjustment needed must be done by twisting or untwisting.   Normally an adjustment of about ½in. can be effected in this way.

As there are only half the number of threads in the loops one would think that this would be a weak spot and lead to breaks, but experience has shown that breakages usually occur at the nocking point, and not at the loops.

All that remains to complete the string is to rub it well with beeswax and then with a piece of leather doubled over, to melt the beeswax into the string.   Also to put the serving on the middle for five or six inches using the same string or thread as for the other serving.   Both these jobs are done with the bow braced.

Before shooting it will, of course, be necessary to mark the nocking point with silk thread or in some other way, making it just thick enough to hold the arrow.

BRACING THE BOW

By placing the lower nock against the left foot, pulling the handle towards your hip with the left hand and pushing the upper nock away from you with the palm of the right hand you should soon learn the knack of slipping the loop into the top nock. (*Illustn.* 1). The distance between the handle and the string when braced should be about 5½in. to 6in. This can be adjusted by the timber hitch.

SERVING THE STRING

Before the bow is used it is wise to " serve " or bind the string with strong thread well waxed.   A different colour from the string looks well.   Start the serving (as at W in Fig. 9) 2in. above the level of the handle when the bow is braced and continue binding in the direction as at " X " for about 6in.   Finish off by pulling the thread back through several loops as at Fig. 9.   This serving will protect the string from wear by the shooting tab and bracer.   It is wise to clean the wax off the surface of the serving which will come into contact with the tab so that it will not stick and prevent a clean loose.   This can be done with a rag dipped in petrol.

It is usual on steel bows to have strings with a loop at each end.   Special precaution must be taken to protect the loops from wear on the steel bow-nocks.   Pieces of thin tough leather bent round the loops and sewn are usually effective.

Arrow Making

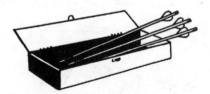

AN arrow must be as straight as possible. Also a set of three or more arrows for target shooting should be as nearly as possible the same weight, the same spine (springiness), and the same balance. To obtain these requirements to perfection takes the professional fletcher all his time and skill. We amateurs can, however, with care, produce quite a satisfactory arrow. If the three we use for target shooting do not fly exactly alike we can number them at the feather end. By continually shooting them we shall soon learn their individual faults and allow for this in our aim. For instance, if No. 3 flies a little more to the left than the first two, then we aim him a little more to the right.

The simplest way to make a serviceable arrow is to obtain from a timber merchant straight birch dowel rods 5/16in. diameter. They are fairly cheap, but the straightest and roundest should be chosen. If slightly bent, they can usually be straightened by hand, but sometimes heat is needed. If you are under 5ft. 6in. you may need 26in. arrows, but over that height 28in. would be best.

After cutting the rod to the correct length, rub it smooth with sandpaper. Now cut the " nock " or notch with three hacksaw blades bolted or tied together ; make sure that the cut is central and across the end grain, as at N in Fig. 3. A cut ¼in. deep is sufficient, rough edges should be cleaned and the end of the shaft rounded with sandpaper.

For a " pile " a bullet-jacket can be used, with the lead melted out and the inside lip filed away. A first-class brass pile (point for target shooting) can be made quite simply from 5/16in. outside diameter brass tubing of 26 gauge with a short length of 9/32in. brass rod sweated into the front end with solder.

Cut a 1in. length of the tubing and ½in. length of the rod ; then, after cleaning carefully with emery to obtain bright metal surfaces to be joined, smear with flux and coat with solder when

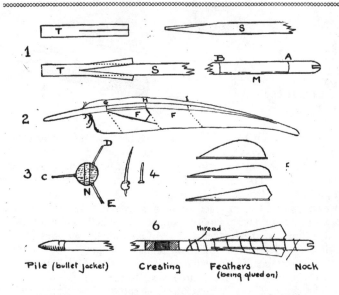

Pile (bullet jacket)   Cresting   Feathers   Nock
                                    (being glued on)

hot. Before the solder cools, insert two-thirds of the rod into the
tube and leave to cool.

A breast-drill or hand-drill held in a vice can be used to spin
the pile while filing it to a point. A piece of bolt with the thread
left on which will screw tightly into the open end of the pile makes
a convenient chuck for holding the pile in the drill whilst filing
and finishing. Emery cloth or sandpaper will give a nice finish
if used while the pile is still turning in the drill.

For a quickly made rough pile take 5/16in. brass or steel
tubing with a large inside diameter. Cut 1in. lengths and,
after fitting on to the shaft straight and flush, carefully insert
a round-headed screw. This is better than too sharp a point for
target shooting, as the penetration is not so great. For odd arrows
to use in " roving " or practise at stumps of trees, etc., the pile
may be formed by tightly binding the end with thin wire for ¾in.
and then inserting a round-head screw. If solder is run over the
wire it makes a stronger job.

All piles are best fitted by using resin. When the shaft has
been carefully shaped to fit right down into the pile, put a few
small pieces of resin in the pile and hold it over the lighted gas until

the resin melts.

Insert the shaft right home and see that it is on straight before the resin cools.   Then clean off surplus resin and polish up the pile with emery.

Best arrows are made from very well-seasoned deal boards with straight grain.   These are sawn into 3/8in. squares an inch or so longer than the required arrow.   Then with a sharp plane each edge is taken off in turn until the shaft is very nearly round. This operation is made easier by using a board or piece of batten, say 30in. long, with a straight V groove cut along it.   A small nail is driven into the groove at one end as a stop.   The square shaft is then placed in the groove and the planing is quite simple.   A hollow, beading plane makes a rounder finish.   The rounding of the shaft is completed with sandpaper.   Nocks and piles are fitted as for birch dowel shafts, except that a piece of fibre should be glued into a sawcut with the grain to strengthen the nock which is cut across the grain.

Deal shafts are rather liable to break if they hit a hard object. It is therefore wise if they are to withstand hard usage to splice on a " footing " of hardwood.   This is not difficult for anyone used to handling tools.   The footing should be of degame or some other straight-grained hardwood.   A piece 8in. long by 3/8in. by 3/8in. is best.   A fine sawcut must be made with the grain, exactly down the centre for $5\frac{1}{2}$in.   A pencil line is then drawn exactly across the centre of the end of the deal shaft, also with the grain.   Then plane a $5\frac{1}{4}$in. taper from each side to the pencil line (S, Fig. 1).   Next bind the footing with a few turns of thread just at end of sawcut to prevent splitting.   Glue the taper and force it into the sawcut, making sure the two shafts line up straight. Bind with cord until the glue is thoroughly dry.   After this, plane off the protruding ears until the footing is the same diameter (5/16in.) as the deal shaft and finish with sandpaper.

Arrows are weighed against new English silver coins.   So a 4s. 6d. arrow does not mean it cost 4s. 6d., but that it weighs the same as four shillings and a sixpence, or a half-crown and a florin.   Arrows suitable for use with a 30lb. (pull) bow should be about 3s. 6d. or 4s., while those for use with a 50lb. bow might need to be as much as 5s. in weight.   Target arrows should be carefully matched in weight by planing wood off the back end before the feathers are fitted.

FLETCHING

The arrow will now require three feathers glued on for steering purposes. This is a rather tricky job to do properly, for naturally if the vanes are not put on right the arrow will not fly straight but will wobble or " flirt." It is wise first to mark out the shaft in pencil, as at M, Fig. 1. A is a line round the shaft about 1¼in. from the end and B a line 2¼in. from A, allowing for feathers 2¼in. long. Three lines should be drawn from A to B straight along the shaft and equal distances apart as at C, D, and E (Fig. 3). so that one feather (C) stands at right-angles to the nock. This is known as the " cock feather," and is usually a different colour from the other two. In shooting, this feather is placed away from the bow so that the others pass without injury.

The best feathers to use are stiff " pinion " or main feathers from the wings of turkeys or geese. These can usually be bought in 3d. and 6d. stores or milliners' shops. There is a difference in the feathers of the right and left wing. The feathers from one side only must be used on an arrow, otherwise it will wobble in flight.

After cutting through the quill at G, H, and I (Fig. 2) it is wise to soften the pieces by placing them between a folded cloth that has been wrung out in hot water. Then place a piece of feather flat on the edge of the bench and, using a flat piece of sheet steel or iron (e.g., steel rule) with a straight edge, place that on the vane and push the quill up flush to it. Then with a sharp knife pare off the quill level with the top surface of the iron plate. Still holding down the feather with the iron, shave off the surplus quill, leaving only 1/16in. strip as a foundation for the vane (see Fig. 4). To make sure the feather will stand straight up on the shaft it is a good plan to grind the base by rubbing on a piece of sandpaper placed flat on the bench. A spring paper-clip is useful for holding the feather while this is done.

These pieces of feather are now stuck on the shaft 1¼in. from the nock end exactly along lines drawn as above (see Figs. 1, 3 and 6). Seccotine is easiest to use. Rub a little on the base and allow it to get tacky before putting feathers in position, then having bound with thread, as in sketch (6), adjust to exact position, lying quite straight along shaft, and leave to dry for 12 hours. When dry, remove thread and trim feathers to the shape you prefer (see sketches (5)) with sharp scissors or razor blade. Be careful to shape the front end of quill down to the shaft so that it does not scratch the hand in shooting.

The quickest and most efficient way of trimming feathers to exactly the same shape is by the use of an electrically heated wire. The fletched arrow is placed in V slots cut in the sides of a box. An electric wire (*e.g.*, part of a fire element) is then bent to the outline of the feather shape required. This cutting wire is then so placed and wired up that when the arrow is turned in the slots each feather is cut to the chosen shape. The wire must be red hot (bright) and it will probably be necessary to wire a two kilowatt electric fire in series with it as a resistance.

It is usual to paint arrows with distinctive bands of colour just in front of the feathers. This is called the " cresting," and each archer should have his own colours so that his arrows can be easily distinguished in the target.

To prevent the glue of the feathers being affected by wet or damp, it is often a good plan to paint between the feathers as well, from the cresting to within 1in. of the nock, taking care not to get paint on the feathers.

TESTING ARROWS FOR SPINE

A simple spine-tester for arrows can be made by inserting two nails in a board far enough apart for one nail to fit in the nock of the arrow while the pile rests on the other nail. This board is then fixed in an upright position and the arrow placed on the two nails with the grain standing vertical. A pound-and-a-half weight is suspended by thread from the arrow half-way between the nails and the amount of deflection read off in tenths and hundredths of an inch on a rule fixed behind centre of arrow.

The following list gives suitable deflections of arrows to be used with bows of the weights given.

	Arrow Weight	Arrow Length	G.N.A.S. Units of Spine or hundredths of an inch deflection.
20 lb. Bow	200-225 grains	26 ins.	90
25 ,, ,,	225-250 ,,	26 ins.	85
30 ,, ,,	250-300 ,,	26 ins.	80
35 ,, ,,	300-350 ,,	26 ins.	75
40 ,, ,,	350-400 ,,	28 ins.	70
45 ,, ,,	400-450 ,,	28 ins.	65
50 ,, ,,	450-500 ,,	28 ins.	60
55 ,, ,,	500-550 ,,	28 ins.	58
60 ,, ,,	550-600 ,,	28 ins.	56

Other

Equipment

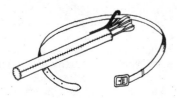

SEVERAL ways of drawing and loosing the bow have been developed by different nations. It appears, however, that the English have always used the three-finger or " Mediterranean " loose. The " pinch " draw of our childhood would of course only be strong enough for toy bows, but the three-finger draw, after practice, gives an excellent loose even with very powerful bows.

With this draw the arrow must be placed on the left side of the bow, and as the three fingers draw the string they should cause the string to roll slightly clockwise, thus tending to keep the arrow against the bow and on the " shelf " formed by the knuckles.

THE TAB

To protect the fingers from the string and also to give a smooth, quick loose, it is necessary to wear a shooting glove, leather finger-stalls, or a tab. The latter is the simplest to make and should be cut out from hard but pliable leather about 1/12th in. thick, having a smooth, polished surface (see Fig. 2). The length can be adjusted to reach just to the end of the fingers, and the slot for the arrow can be cut deeper if required. By first cutting a brown paper pattern to fit the hand you may avoid cutting the leather the wrong size.

Some archers use grease on the tab to allow the string to slip off easily, others prefer French chalk for that purpose.

THE BRACER

To protect the left arm from the recoil of the string and to keep sleeves, etc., from catching or deflecting the string, it is wise to wear a bracer. This can be made of fairly stiff leather and fastened on with straps or holes punched on the edges and leather laces or tapes arranged for tying. In whatever way it is fixed, care must be taken to see that no obstruction is on the surface of the bracer likely to come in contact with the string.

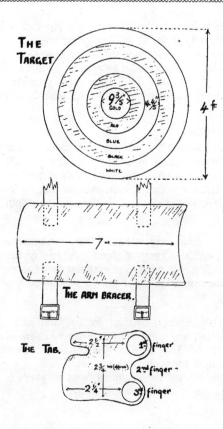

TASSEL

Keep arrows clean; mud on them affects their flight. A tassel made of wool is usually hung on the belt and is used to wipe any arrows hitting the ground. Failing that, a piece of rag should be kept in your pocket for the purpose.

THE QUIVER

Most archers, especially ladies, find it convenient to use a quiver to hold the arrows while shooting. Men can hold them in hip or trouser pockets, but they are not usually so conveniently placed as in a quiver.

A simple quiver can be made from a piece of pliable leather or other suitable material about 17in. long and 7in. wide. Holes can be punched along the sides and lower edge so that it can then be sewn with leather thongs into a cylindrical tube, a circle of similar leather being sewn into the bottom. To complete the quiver a leather loop should be sewn to the top with which it can be attached to the belt.

GROUND QUIVER

A " ground quiver " which acts as a stand for the arrows and bow can be made from a piece of iron rod about 2ft. 6ins. long. One end is filed to a point while the other is bent into a ring of about 4ins. diameter. This is bent over so that when the point is stuck in the ground the circle holds the arrows upright.

BOW CASE

It is also a good plan to have a cloth or waterproof case for your bow, in which to carry it about. A strip of black or green cloth will do. Sew it down one side and at the bottom, with a flap and tape at the top; after the style of a fishing-rod case.

THE TARGET

The regulation target as used in England and America is 48 in. in diameter, and consists of a centre 9.3/5 in. diameter, and four rings each 4.4/5 in. wide. The centre is coloured gold and the rings red, light blue, black and white.

This target is used for distances from 40 yards to 100 yards. For shorter ranges a smaller target is used.

Target Making

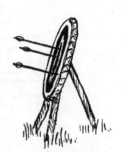

IT is laborious, but not difficult, to make one's own target, provided good straw can be obtained, either from a farmer or the local corn-chandler. A ball or two of medium thin but strong string will also be needed and a packing needle.

The method is first to make a continuous rope of straw about 3 in. in diameter, compressed and bound as tightly as possible with the string. This operation is helped considerably by using a wooden funnel. It should be about a foot long, tapering from about 6 in. at the large end to 3 in. at the small. The straw is fed in continuously at the large end and pulled out and wound with string at the small end. The taper of the funnel compresses the rope to the right thickness.

Having prepared the straw rope the next step is to twist it into a tight flat disc. The first turn can be four or five inches and as each turn is made it should be sewn to the previous turn with the packing needle and string.

When sufficient turns have been completed to give the required width (*i.e.,* just over two feet for the smallest international target), the " rope " should be tapered off and sewn down flush with the outer edge. The wearing qualities of the boss depend to a great extent upon how tightly each turn is sewn down to the previous turn.

Standard 4 feet targets can, of course, be made in this way, but need about four times the amount of straw rope and considerably more effort.

After the target face has been painted with the usual colours on strong canvas, it should be cut circular and sewn by its outside edge to the boss.

Targets of this type, will, of course, need a wooden stand to

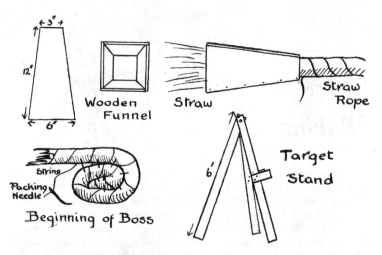

hold them at such a height that the centre is 4 feet from the ground. It is best to use softwood boards for the stand. If 6 feet boards are used the stand will do for either 4 ft. or 2 ft. targets.

Three 6 ft. boards are used and 4 in. by 1 in. is quite suitable. A large hole should be drilled through each board at the top, through which a long carriage bolt should fit very loosely. This must allow the three boards to separate at the bottom and form a tripod.

On the two front legs of the tripod short pieces of the same material are screwed at right angles to the leg with about six inches projecting forward. These must be put at such a height that when the target is rested upon them the centre will be four feet from the ground.

The target should be further secured to the stand by a loop of string attached to the top of the target, and thrown over the top of the stand. If there is likely to be any wind, it is a wise precaution to put a screw-eye into the bottom of the back leg of the stand, through which a long skewer or stake can be pushed into the ground. This will prevent the target being blown forward — a very annoying thing if you happen to have all your best arrows in it at the time!

Shooting Technique

W HEN you have made your bow, some arrows, a tab for your fingers, and a bracer for your arm, you will be ready to go out and try your equipment and your skill (or lack of it!) in shooting. If possible, for a start, find some " wide open space " when no one is about and shoot at a fair elevation. A bow shoots its farthest when the arrow makes an angle of 45 deg. with the ground. However, make quite sure no one is in the way and that the field is large enough for you not to lose your arrow.

It's a grand sight to watch a good arrow streak through the air for 100—200 yards or more. This is especially true if you have made both bow and arrow yourself.

If no open space is available, shoot at some kind of butt or grassy bank.

Good, accurate shooting depends on close attention to a few details. Roger Ascham, who wrote his famous book on Archery called "Toxophilus" in 1545, named his five points thus: "Standyng, nockyng, drawyng, holdyng, lowsyng, done as they shoulde be done, make fayre shootynge."

Although we no longer spell them in quite the same way, the same actions need careful attention; with the possible addition of two more — looking and pausing. It is the careful practice of each of these details until they become automatically right that will eventually make you a good shot with the possibility of not only becoming Club Champion and County Champion, but later on British Champion, with a trip abroad to shoot for this country in International Matches.

STANDING

If there is a line or mark from which to shoot, archers place one foot on either side of it. FEET SHOULD BE COMFORT-

ABLY APART but not too wide. FACE EXACTLY AT RIGHT-
ANGLES TO THE TARGET AND ONLY TURN THE HEAD
left TOWARDS THE TARGET in shooting. In this way the two
shoulders and toes will line up with the target. (*Illustn.* 2).

NOCKING

Having taken your " stance," hold the strung bow horizon-
tally in your left hand down by your side, string uppermost. Now
bend your bow-arm at the elbow and bring the hand and bow up
level with the hip — very nearly in the " hips firm " position but
with the hand grasping bow and with the string on the forearm near
the elbow. With the bow in this position it is simple to take an
arrow (it is quite usual to carry target arrows in a right-hand pocket)
in the right hand and " nock " it on the string. It is passed underneath the bow and pushed on to the " nocking point " of the string.
This point should be just above the level of the handle when the
bow is held upright and should be previously marked by thread
bound round, over the serving for about 3/8 in. and made sufficiently thick just to hold the arrow from dropping off.

Having nocked the arrow with the cock feather outwards from
the bow, the left arm is straightened again and the three " drawing "
fingers of the right hand placed on the string. FIRST FINGER
ABOVE AND SECOND AND THIRD FINGERS BELOW THE
ARROW WITHOUT TOUCHING IT! (*Illustns.* 3-6).

LOOKING

Before drawing it is a wise habit to look at the target and
DETERMINE JUST EXACTLY WHAT SPOT TO AIM AT,
bearing in mind which arrow of the set you are using and its faults,
if any. (*Illustn.* 6, 10 *and* 11).

Now check your grip of the bow. In the old days the bow was
always gripped tightly, and some of the best archers still use that
method, keeping the back of the hand in line with the wrist and
the base joint of the thumb directly behind the handle.

A careful study of the photographs will show you how the bow
should be held in the more modern relaxed method, with just
sufficient hold to keep the bow from falling. The arrow must pass
just above the handle and across the knuckles, which act as a shelf.

DRAWING

Without taking your eyes off the target, steadily straighten out and lift the bow-arm and draw back the string hand, keeping the rear elbow high. DRAW THE STRING BACK UNTIL IT TOUCHES THE CENTRE OF THE CHIN while the face is turned towards the target) and THE FIRST FINGER IS JUST BELOW BUT TOUCHING THE CHIN. Great care should be taken to draw to the same place each time. (*Illustns.* 7-9).

To make sure that the head is not thrown back but is held upright it is a good habit to touch the nose to the string.

It is an excellent practice to breathe in fairly deeply as you draw, and hold the breath until you have loosed. This helps a steady aim and develops the chest — a splendid open-air exercise in these days of lung trouble.

HOLDING

This should only be long enough to aim. There are several ways of aiming but the simplest for target shooting is to place a piece of $\frac{1}{8}$ in. adhesive tape round the bow at about 5 in. above the handle (*i.e.*, about the same as the distance between chin and eye). If you draw to the chin as above directed, you then AIM WITH THE RIGHT EYE (closing the left if this helps), lining up the left edge of the tape with the target while the bow is held quite upright. If the arrows fly left, aim to right of target. A tape 5 in. or so up the bow should do for any distance up to 20 yards. For 30 yards it may have to be $3\frac{1}{2}$ in. from handle. This can be discovered and adjusted by experience. (*Illustn.* 9-11).

LOOSING

While the aim is steady on the mark, allow the string to slip off the fingers without allowing them to " creep " forward. If the string is held about half way between the tips and the first joints this will not be difficult. Everything else being correct, the success of the shot depends on a clean, smooth loose. The wearing of a " tab " or shooting-glove not only prevents blisters, but helps a SMOOTH, SHARP LOOSE. (*Illustn.* 12).

PAUSING

The exact position upon loosing should be held until the arrow hits the target (or the ground, if it's your " off day "). This will tend to prevent any jerking of the bow or string before the arrow leaves and helps you to correct any faults next time. (*Illustn.* 13).

If you learn by heart the above instructions in capitals, it will be simple to check yourself up while shooting.

It is wise to begin target shooting at 10 yards. When you can group the arrows fairly well, then go back to 20 yards and later to 30 yards. In competition rounds, however, the longer distances are always shot first.

SCORING

Archers never speak of the bullseye, but always of the gold. This counts 9, the red 7, blue 5, black 3, and white 1. Any arrow cutting a higher colour counts as a hit in that colour.

As arrows are shot in a series of six, which is called an " end," scoring books or cards are ruled up in columns so that the score of each of the six arrows can be entered in one column. Additional columns are ruled for the number of hits on the target made by the half-dozen arrows, the total score for the half-dozen, and the number of golds obtained.

In competition shooting, arrows must not be removed from the target until they have been recorded by the scorer; thus avoiding dispute.

However much of a novice you may be for a time, directly you begin to hit the target at all start keeping your score. This will enable you to watch your progress. You will see that little by little you are improving your score and making better groups on the target in spite of many disappointments.   Also it will encourage you to watch for and correct faults in technique in order to beat your last top score.

The score sheet of the British Record York Round, on the old system of scoring, will be found on page 12.

Illn. 1. BRACING (stringing) the Bow.

Putting pressure at three points with the bow against the left foot pull left hand and push right until the loop can be slipped into the nock with the free fingers of right hand. Not as inset.

Illn. 2. STANDING (stance).

Upright and at right angles to the target. Only the head is turned left while shooting. Not as inset.

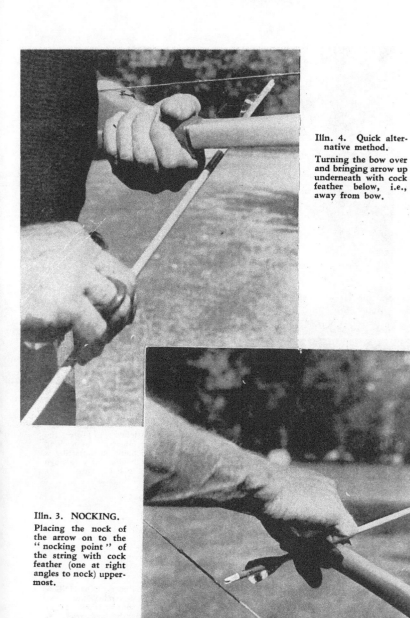

Illn. 4. Quick alternative method.

Turning the bow over and bringing arrow up underneath with cock feather below, i.e., away from bow.

Illn. 3. NOCKING.

Placing the nock of the arrow on to the "nocking point" of the string with cock feather (one at right angles to nock) uppermost.

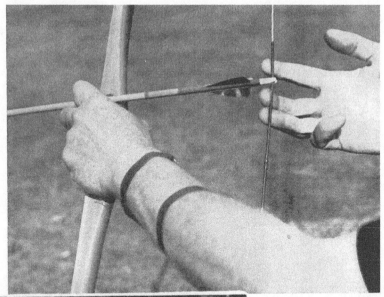

Illn. 5.
First finger above and 2nd and 3rd fingers below arrow, without touching it. Known as the "Mediterranean Loose." Normally, a leather "tab" is worn to protect the fingers. The nocking point on the string is bound large enough to hold arrow.

Illn. 6. LOOKING to determine the exact spot at which to aim, with bow ready to draw.

The Steel Bow in use.

Illn. 7.
DRAWING with relaxed (or loose) hold on bow, arrow just above handle.

Illn. 8.
String is drawn back to the centre of the chin, first finger pushed up under chin. This is called the "anchor point." Right elbow held high.

Not with hunched shoulder, low elbow and aiming along arrow.

Illn. 9. HOLDING at full draw momentarily while aim is taken.
Left eye closed as in rifle shooting if this helps.

Illn. 10. AIMING is accomplished by lining up the tip of the arrow with some natural mark on the ground called the " point of aim." Practice and experiment teaches just where this point is located for different distances.

Illn. 11.
Another method of aiming is to use a mark or movable band on the bow, lining this up with the centre of the target. Or if arrows are flying left, to the right of centre.

Illn. 12. LOOSING. The hand held steady against the chin.

Illn. 13. PAUSING while remaining in the exact position of loose until the arrow hits the target.

Avoid dropping bow arm as inset.

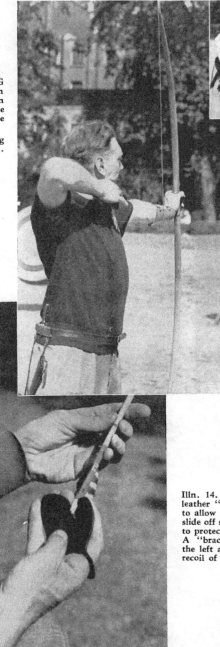

Illn. 14. A polished leather "tab" is used to allow the string to slide off smoothly and to protect the fingers. A "bracer" protects the left arm from the recoil of the string.

Safety First

THOSE who have watched modern archery or made and used the equipment described in previous chapters, will have realised that these are by no means toys to be handled carelessly. To prevent annoyance and danger to others, certain rules must be rigidly observed while shooting.

Never shoot straight up. A slight wind may bring the arrow back on to yourself or spectators near you.

Never point a drawn bow at anyone, even in fun.

When long-distance shooting on public ground, have a safety man as far away as the arrows are likely to fall and well to one side. His job is to stop the shooting by a prearranged signal should anyone come within range.

The recognised warning among archers to let others know that one is wanting to shoot, when they might be in the way, is the cry of " Fast!", similar to the use of " Fore!" in golf. This gave rise to the phrase, " to play fast and loose " which meant to cry " Fast!" and loose before others had time to get out of the way — that is, to act carelessly and dangerously.

When target shooting make sure that no one is behind or near the target. The best way is to insist that all those watching must stand well behind those actually shooting; this avoids the danger of a glancing shot. It also avoids distracting the archer. This is important in competition shooting.

For the archer's own safety he should be careful never to draw the arrow " within " the bow. That is to overdraw it so that the pile catches on the inside of the bow. If he should loose with the arrow in this position it will splinter and may injure his hand or face. It is therefore better to have an arrow too long for you than too short.

SAFETY OF YOUR EQUIPMENT

Keep strings and the serving on them in good order. A broken string may allow the bow to recoil too fast and break the bow. For the same reason a bow should never be drawn or loosed without an arrow on the string.

Never leave a bow or arrows lying on the ground. They are likely to get damp or be trodden on and both are detrimental. If you need to shoot in the rain, dry your tackle thoroughly afterwards and then rub over with a little linseed oil on a rag.

Should your bow develop a " shake " or fine split running lengthways, bind for an inch or two with strong thread, and then varnish. This will often keep such a bow from breaking.

Be careful how you draw arrows from the target or the ground, otherwise they are liable to get badly bent in the process.

Four should be the maximum number shooting on a target together. Otherwise the shooting line is too crowded and there is great danger of hitting one another's arrows. If therefore more than four wish to shoot and there is only one target, the first four should remove their arrows from the target while others are preparing to shoot.

Archery Golf

A FAVOURITE game of the old English bowmen was called Rovers. It consisted of roving through the fields picking any distant and suitable mark such as a tree, tree stump, molehill, log or post. The archer hitting nearest to the object was the winner of that " mark." The arrows were then retrieved and another mark chosen.

The game was so popular that eventually certain fields were set apart and permanent marks erected, each given its name and set at varied distances from the other marks. Examples of such Roving courses were the Finsbury Fields north of Moorgate, and Shooters Hill, near South London.

Several authorities hold that Golf was adapted from this archery game of Rovers. We archers certainly can't blame the golfers for copying this grand outdoor exercise.

A similar game to Rovers which makes a welcome change from target practice is now called Archery Golf. There are several varieties of this sport, and it is very simple to arrange provided open fields, or better still a golf course (with permission) can be used.

Simple rules for the game are as follows:—

1. Any bow may be used except a cross-bow.

2. Two or more arrows of any weight, one fitted with a long point (to prevent bouncing off turf when " putting ").

3. " Holes " are 4 in. discs of white cardboard fitted into a cut in a stick and stuck into the ground with the top not more than one foot from the ground.

4. Any number of " holes " up to nine may be placed at varying distances (preferably over 200 yards apart) the next hole being clearly visible from the previous one.

5. Archers (any number) may shoot their first arrow (at each hole) together. From behind the spot where that arrow falls they

shoot again, the archer with the arrow shortest of the mark shooting first.

6. Each arrow shot counts one point. The archer completing the course (out nine holes and back nine holes or as arranged) in the least number of shots wins.

7. An archer completes a " hole " by hitting the disc (which may be turned to face him) or by hitting the ground within two yards (bow length) of the disc. In the latter case he must take two points and reckon to have completed that " hole."

A match between an archer and a golfer makes a very interesting and usually a close game. With practice most " holes " can be completed in three shots.

When " putting " on a golf course it is advisable to use an arrow with a long spike as ordinary target arrows are prone to bounce off the turf of a putting green when shot at a low angle.

Flight Shooting

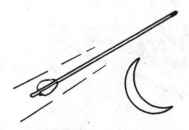

FLIGHT shooting is concerned only with distance and pays very little attention to accuracy of aim. It becomes an absorbing hobby for those who take it up as it involves experimenting with the material and design of bows in order to get the utmost cast possible from the material. This applies also to the arrows used and the special technique in shooting them.

Mr. Ingo Simon is the leading authority on flight shooting in England. He has found that the short Turkish type bow composed of horn, wood and sinew casts further than any other type. It is made by gluing a horn belly to a thin wood foundation and backing this with sinew fibres under tension. The long rigid " ears " that take the place of the tips on a longbow, give sufficient leverage to enable the extremely short and strong " working " part of the limb to be drawn.

Light arrows are used of course, but they must be rigid enough to withstand the very fast recoil of the bow. With this in view most flight arrows are tapered from just in front of the feathers to a very small light pile. The feathers too are extremely small and cut low to lessen wind resistance. To minimise friction through the air and against the bow many flight archers lubricate the arrow with graphite or other lubricant and use a special rest on the bow.

The record flight shot by English archers still stands at 462 yards 9 inches, and was shot by Mr. Ingo Simon at Le Touquet on June 26th, 1914.

American flight archers are now following the design of the Turkish bow and are regularly reaching distances well over 600 yards with hand bows. Using a very heavy bow fixed across the feet and pulled by both hands while lying on the back or by what is called " free style " distances up to 700 yards have been reached.

As far as we know the world's flight record was a shot of 975

yards by a Turkish Sultan way back in the 18th century. This is
by no means based on mere tradition as are Robin Hood's long
shots. In the Turkish case pillars were erected marking the distance
and the inscription can be read today.

At the present rate of progress, especially in America, it is quite
feasible that archers will again reach these astounding distances.

In any case those who have been trying have rendered a great
service to archery in general as their researches in bow and arrow
design have led to much improvement in the efficiency of our
modern tackle.

Hunting

B ow hunting for big game is now a thing of the past in England, but in the United States it is gaining many adherents. The authorities are also recognising the advantages of bow-hunting, and in many States are setting aside special " seasons " for this type of hunting only. The comparative silence of the bow does not disturb the game in a wide area, and provided the hunter is a good stalker he can get more shots than a rifleman in the same area.

A moderately strong bow, between fifty and eighty pounds, is used for big game. The old English broadhead type of arrow is generally used and when the cutting edges are sharp the penetrating power of this arrow is very great. In Britain there is no game that would warrant the use of these broadheads, except perhaps the deer on the Scottish Highlands if one could get near enough to them in such open country.

Small game shooting, however, can be a very exciting sport, and a reasonably good shot should often bring home something to show for his patient stalking.

The best practice for small game shooting is target archery followed by short range roving at small objects (tufts of grass, etc.) in order to learn to judge distances accurately.

Big game hunters aim instinctively without the use of any sighting device. Their target is large and seldom gives them time to use a sight. The writer, however, has found the best method with small game, such as rabbits, etc., is to use a sight which can be quickly set at the most likely distances (20 yards, 30 yards, 40 yards) and then rely on careful stalking to give sufficient time to judge the distance and set the sight. If the hunter's arrows do not fly left he can use a rubber ring and plain marks on the bow. If they do fly much to the left, however, he would be better advised to use a piece of cork glued to the back of his bow, and a pin standing at right angles. Having judged the distance he can sight the pinhead right on the game.

The best arrows to use for this type of rabbit shooting are reliable target arrows. Four or five that group together are an advantage. But one should not use one's best target arrows as they so easily get lost in hunting, unless great care is taken to watch where they fall, and this is rarely done in the excitement.

The whole object of stalking is, of course, to get as close as possible to the quarry without disturbing it. In the case of rabbits, slow, silent approach is the chief necessity. Their long ears quickly pick up the slightest unnatural sound and they warn all their neighbours by sharp taps on the ground with their hind legs. When a rabbit is suspicious of some sound he will usually sit upright with his ears up. If you see him in this position your best chance is to stand perfectly still in the hope that he has not seen you, and will soon forget his fears and drop on to his front paws again to feed. Then you can try again. The slightest move while he is watching will send him scampering for his hole, and all others within sight will follow suit.

Having previously located the haunt of rabbits you are most likely to find them out of their holes at sunrise or sunset. It is then best to approach them by creeping along the hedge in the next field, provided there are gaps in it sufficient to shoot through. If possible move in the direction so that your bow-arm is nearest the hedge. This will mean that you need only show your bow and head when shooting through a gap. If the first arrow misses crouch down silently and after a while take another careful look. The chances are that the arrow only scared the rabbit momentarily, and it may only be a few yards away from its original position, so allowing an adjustment of the sight and another shot.

For shooting grey squirrels, rooks and any other pests in trees it is advisable to use arrows fitted with a hardwood knob in place of the target pile. The latter tends to stick in the tree in the case of a miss and means a climb to retrieve the arrow. These knobs or blunts can be made from $1\frac{1}{2}$ in. of birch dowel rod, about $\frac{3}{4}$ in. dia. drilled to take the shaft and rounded at the front, or carved pear-shape. At close range these deliver a blow sufficient to stun or kill small game, but will bounce off if they hit a branch of the tree itself.

It is hardly necessary to say that when hunting it is unwise to wear bright or light colours. Something that tones in naturally with the surroundings is best.

Also have an arrow ready on the string always and keep a careful eye ahead, otherwise many chances may be missed.

Improving Scores

W ITH a bow not too strong to be held steady throughout the round and with reasonably straight and matched arrows, it is possible for an archer to make fair scores at distances up to say 60 yards, provided of course he has practised good technique until each action from the stance to the loose has become second nature.

If, however, he aspires to make really high scores, there are other factors that must be considered. Success in archery consists of reducing every possible variable to a constant, but there are some variables which cannot be reduced. Wind and weather have their effect on scores. so have the nervous tension of the archer, the condition of his health and the fatigue of his drawing fingers and bow arm.

When using a strong bow, moderate wind does not have much effect up to 60 yards range, but at 80 yards and 100 yards, even a light wind has its effect. A cross wind must of course be allowed for, by having the point of aim more to the right (or left) at one end than at the other.

A following wind is most disconcerting, and usually makes it necessary to alter the point of aim, as compared with a head wind, sometimes in reverse of what would be expected. All this makes it advisable to note anything that will indicate the direction and force of the wind before shooting the longer distances. Smoke from chimneys, leaves of trees, swaying grass, etc., may forewarn the archer and save those few points which sometimes make all the difference in a tournament. Care must be taken, however, not to make too much allowance for wind. It is the writer's opinion that the wind gets blamed for more than it really deserves.

On the other hand, the general weather conditions have an

On the Target . . .

With all types of archery equipment and suitable clothing, Lillywhites give valuable advice to the beginner and a specialised service for the more experienced. Please write for price list giving full details ; some examples are given below :—

THE GALLOWAY BOW *(illustrated near right)* A new departure in English bow technique ; made by Mr. Richard Galloway of Scotland, these bows are recurved or retroflexed and made up in laminations of high quality woods. Each £7.15.10.

STEEL BOWS *(illustrated far right).* Increasingly popular, sound in design, consistent in accuracy in any climate. Two piece bows available in weights up to 45 lbs. £8.11.1.

TOURNAMENT ARROWS Made from finest seasoned timber, guaranteed matched in weight and spine. Each 11/- Practice Bows from 42/- Practice Arrows from 2/6

Supplies of Apollo Arrows made from Hiduminium tubing by Accles & Pollock are extremely limited and at the present time for export only.

effect upon wood bows, wood arrows and linen strings, which is not always appreciated and allowed for. Warm moist days appear to cause a slackening in all three, which together can cause arrows to drop appreciably short. Also because of slight alteration in the spine of the arrow and the speed of cast of the bow, lateral adjustment of the point of aim may be needed. If a record is kept on a stick or a piece of card, or better still on a piece of perspex, of the points of aim at certain distances with a particular bow and set of arrows, then care should be taken to ascertain any needed alteration for at least one distance before using these points of aim in a tournament on another day. The alteration needed at one distance will indicate very nearly that needed at all distances. The same considerations and allowances apply of course when a mark on the bow is used for aiming instead of a point of aim on the ground.

If steel bows, steel arrows and steel strings are used, very little alteration in the point of aim is needed because of altered weather conditions. Also steel arrows, having a small diameter, appear to be affected less by the wind than arrows of a similar weight in deal or Port Orford cedar.

The co-ordination between nerve and muscle plays a big part in archery. Therefore anything which affects the nervous system, whether excitement or bad habits, will have an effect on scores, as witness the usually much higher scores made in the quiet of private practice, compared with those made before a " gallery " or in an important tournament. On these occasions it is also much harder to achieve the required concentration at the moment of the aim and loose. Spectators do not very often realise the need for this concentration, and thoughtlessly distract the archer's attention at the vital moment. Then if the arrow does not fly true, they blame the archer instead of themselves.

In a tournament, where a double York or double Hereford is being shot, care must be taken to prevent over-tiring the drawing fingers and the bow arm. An endeavour should be made completely to rest these muscles while not actually shooting. The habit of allowing the arms to hang loosely while walking and waiting to shoot between ends is some help.

The relaxed method of shooting saves a good deal of fatigue in the arms. In this method the bow is not gripped tightly, and the drawing fingers remain almost straight except for the end phalanges which are just sufficiently bent to retain the string.

ARCHERY

The sport with a future

The men who today make *F.H.Ayres* Archery equipment draw heavily on more than 100 years' experience of the craft. But like archery itself, they are always ready to take advantage of new methods and new materials.

So it is that the modern archer, using modern equipment, can outstrip the achievement of the archer of history and is always looking ahead to further records.

SLAZENGER *F.H.Ayres* REGD. ARCHERY EQUIPMENT

The whole body has its part in the act of drawing rather than merely the arms. The fatigue being thus shared, is greatly reduced. It is also a help to take a moderately deep breath while drawing; this breath is then held to enable a steady aim and loose to be accomplished.

Although good tackle by no means makes a good archer, yet it is equally true that a good archer cannot shoot his best unless he uses reliable tackle. By far the most important part of the equipment is the set of arrows. However well made these may be, there are sure to be some which fly outside the general group made by the others, and to save having to make too much altera- tion in aim for each individual arrow, it is wise to use those which make the closest group. The best plan when sorting new arrows, is to number each one temporarily in pencil, then decide on a very distinct aiming point. Taking great care to aim each arrow at this point, shoot off the whole set at say 40 yards. Whether you shoot into the ground which should be soft turf, or whether you choose to shoot into a target, makes no difference, so long as in the former case a wooden peg is placed in the ground roughly in the centre of the group, for future reference.

The next step is to plot the position of the arrows by their numbers on a piece of paper. Repeat two or three times, shoot- ing the whole set from the same spot at the same aiming point, and plot each time the positions of all arrows in reference to the gold or the peg in the ground.

Even allowing for errors on the part of the archer himself, it will soon be found that certain arrows are consistently grouping together. The seven (six and one spare) that make the closest group should be selected for tournament work, and permanently numbered one to seven, and the others may be made up into addi- tional groups with consecutive numbers. These first seven can then be relied upon to group well when shot from the same bow. Another bow may cause them to group in quite a different manner of course. Also, any injury to the arrows will very often alter the grouping, so that the tournament set should be used with care. It should be borne in mind that sometimes arrows which group well at say 80 yards, may not group at all well, comparatively, at 50 yards, so that careful note should be taken of the performance of a set of arrows at the distances expected to be shot.

A further word may be in place here regarding the spine of

the arrows. It has been shown by a series of high speed photographs that the sudden force exerted upon the nock of the arrow when it is loosed tends to bend the arrow more or less, according to its stiffness and the speed with which the bow recoils. It is obvious that if it bent first one way (with the back away from the bow) then when it recovers and bends the other way owing to the springiness or spine of the arrow wood, part of the arrow is bound to strike against the bow, unless the arrow has passed the bow before the reverse buckle takes place. It therefore follows that the spine of the arrows needs to suit the speed of cast of the bow, otherwise the " slap " of some part of the arrows on the bow will deflect them and make it necessary to use an aiming point to the right, or sometimes the left, of the target.

Although this deflection of the arrows may be fairly constant, and not affect the scoring very much, yet it is an advantage to have an aiming point on or in line with the gold. Fortunate is the archer therefore, who finds a good set of arrows whose spine is suited to his bow. The best tackle makers are now marking arrows with a " spine number " and can advise on the correct spine to be used with any " weight " of bow.

The stiffness of an arrow is fairly simple to measure, and as stiffness is one of the factors in " spine," good fletchers who recognise its importance make sets of arrows with a matched stiffness.

WHERE YOU CAN BUY

If you think of buying:—

WEATHERPROOFS, OVERCOATS, SUITS, UNDERWEAR, PYJAMAS, TIES, SOCKS, CASHMERE SWEATERS, and other apparel of RICH QUALITY, CHOICE and BEAUTIFUL DESIGNS and MATERIALS, you will be DE-LIGHTED, SATISFIED, and find the TIME WELL SPENT by a visit to BURBERRYS, where you will receive the ATTENTION and POLITENESS of an OLD WORLD FIRM with NEW WORLD PRODUCTIONS.

These articles can be bought free of purchase tax, for mailing to your home address, or for delivery to your port of embarkation

BURBERRYS

HAYMARKET, LONDON, S.W.1.

Telephone: WHITEHALL 3343

BURBERRYS LTD.

EQUIPMENT FOR ALL SPORTS

Between the Draw and the Loose

14th century.

THE space of time between the completion of the draw and the loose is very brief, yet many an archer's shooting is spoiled by faults developed at that moment. This is very often caused by the use of a bow stronger than can be comfortably managed, or by the muscles becoming tired through continued shooting. There is a slight and very often unconscious relaxing of the tension in either the bow-arm or the drawing arm resulting in the arrow creeping forward from full draw, and thus weakening the shot.

The best cure for this trouble is to concentrate on getting the elbow of the drawing arm well back and thus opening the chest and pulling the shoulder blades together at the back. If this fails, a weaker bow should be used.

Similar to " creeping " is the " forward loose " where not only the fingers are relaxed in the act of loosing but the arm is allowed to come forward as well. To counter this, the arm should be drawn back slowly in loosing, pulling the string hard into the chin. Any tendency to jerk however must be avoided.

Although the time of " holding " before the loose should not vary and should not be so long as to tire the muscles, yet it should allow sufficient time for the aim to be held steadily until the loose is complete. To loose while the aim is moving across the target can never lead to consistently high scores.

If an archer shoots with a more or less rigid bow-arm there is a danger, when the arrow is loosed, of that arm swinging out of line. Any movement will be sideways as the arm cannot be further stretched. Sometimes this movement happens before the arrow has left the bow and so deflects the arrow. If on the other hand the elbow of the bow arm is slightly flexed, when the arrow is released there is a natural " follow through " in the direction of the target, thus avoiding a deflection.

Assuming that an archer brings his " sight " (mark on bow or other device) down on to the target, it sometimes happens that he

develops the bad habit of continuing that downward movement in
the form of a jerk after the loose or even simultaneous with the
loose. If he brings his sight up on to the target the jerk may develop in the upward direction, in either case spoiling the scores. A
conscious pressing of the bow towards the target at the moment of
the loose often helps to cure this habit.

A psychological trouble that sometimes affects archers who do
a lot of shooting is known as " target shyness." The one so afflicted
finds it extremely difficult and sometimes impossible to bring the
sight on to the chosen mark although he may get fairly near it
with ease. It appears that the muscles will not budge that extra
fraction of an inch. The best cure known to the writer is to have
it well in mind that some additional thing must be done after aiming. Strangely enough in most cases, a perfect aim can then be
taken with ease and the additional action completed before the
loose. If the arrow is not quite fully drawn the additional action
can be the completion of the draw very steadily after the aim.

Some archers prefer to shoot with both eyes open and this is
no doubt an advantage at the longer ranges. Care however must be
taken to form the habit of only using the left hand image of the
bow (which is out of focus) when aiming with both eyes open. For
shooting at less than 50 yards, however, closing the left eye (with
right-hand archers) seems to give a sharper aim.

Should arrows, because of incorrect spine, be flying to the left,
this can be partly corrected by " opening the bow window " as it is
called. Normally one lines up the left-hand side of the string image
(which is a blur, out of focus) and the bow with the aiming point.
If, however, the right side of the string image is used, a gap is formed
between the string and the bow, and the point of aim is viewed in
that gap or " window." This has the advantage of pointing the
arrow a little further to the right, but great care must be taken to see
that the " window " is opened to the same extent at each shot.

The foregoing will no doubt incline us to agree with the well-
known author and yachtsman, Weston Martyr, when he writes
in " Wandering Years," " When a friend suggested archery, I
said: ' But bows and arrows is just a kid's game; my friend said,
' Oh, is it? You try.' I did try, and found I was tackling the
most difficult game I had ever attacked. Presently it dawned
on me that to consistently shoot arrows straight, demanded more
knowledge, eye judgment, determination, nerve, strength, thought,

and practice than racing a boat to windward in a breeze of wind. So I became an archer; and as I have made up my mind never to give up archery until I have mastered it, it is clear I will remain an archer to the end of my days. To shoot a straight arrow is chiefly a matter of intellect. More brain than muscle is needed. It is fine exercise for the body, but better than that, it gives the brain a deal of delightful and stimulating food for thought. The care and repair of the gear is a charming business. The materials an archer works with are wood, leather, feathers and flax."

BIBLIOGRAPHY

TOXOPHILUS	*Roger Ascham*	1544
THEORY AND PRACTICE OF ARCHERY	*Horace Ford*	1860
" ARCHERY " IN THE BADMINTON LIBRARY	*C. J. Longman Col. Walrond and others.*	1894
ARCHERY	*Dr. Robert Elmer U.S.A.*	1926
MODERN ARCHERY	*A. Lambert U.S.A.*	1929
BOWS AND ARROWS	*James Duff U.S.A.*	1941
NEW ARCHERY	*Paul Gordon U.S.A.*	1943
TARGET ARCHERY	*Dr. Robert Elmer U.S.A.*	1946
AN ARCHER'S NOTES	*C. B. Edwards England*	1949